THE SPIRITUAL
SIGNIFICANCE
OF EATING

I0151161

THE SPIRITUAL SIGNIFICANCE OF EATING

GIANFRANCO CARDINAL RAVASI

A Crossroad Book
The Crossroad Publishing Company

The Crossroad Publishing Company
www.CrossroadPublishing.com

© 2017 by The Crossroad Publishing Company

Crossroad, Herder & Herder, and the crossed C logo/colophon
are registered trademarks of The Crossroad Publishing Company.

All rights reserved. No part of this book may be copied, scanned,
reproduced in any way, or stored in a retrieval system, or transmit-
ted, in any form or by any means, electronic, mechanical, photo-
copying, recording, or otherwise, without the written permission
of The Crossroad Publishing Company. For permission please
write to rights@crossroadpublishing.com

In continuation of our 200-year tradition of independent publishing, The Crossroad Publishing Company proudly offers a variety
of books with strong, original voices and diverse perspectives. The
viewpoints expressed in our books are not necessarily those of
The Crossroad Publishing Company, any of its imprints or of its
employees, executives, owners. Although the author and publisher
have made every effort to ensure that the information in this book
was correct at press time, the author and publisher do not assume
and hereby disclaim any liability to any party for any loss, damage,
or disruption caused by errors or omissions, whether such errors
or omissions result from negligence, accident, or any other cause.
No claims are made or responsibility assumed for any health or
other benefits.

Library of Congress Cataloging-in-Publication Data
available from the Library of Congress.

ISBN 978-0-8245-2182-0

Books published by The Crossroad Publishing Company may be
purchased at special quantity discount rates for classes and insti-
tutional use. For information, please e-mail sales@Crossroad
Publishing.com.

ISBN 978-0-8245-0187-7 (epub)

CONTENTS

INTRODUCTION

In his *Domestic Breviary* (1927), the famous German playwright Berthold Brecht noted ironically that "For the high-born, talking about food is a lowly thing. But of course, they've already eaten." In the religious tradition drawn from the Bible, on the other hand, with its concern for history and the Incarnation, food is acknowledged to be a major component of earthly existence. Indeed, one of the first statements God makes to human beings, his creatures, concerns eating: "And God said, 'Behold, I have given you every plant yielding seed which is upon the face of all the earth, and every tree with seed in its fruit; you shall have them for food. . . .' And the LORD God commanded the man, saying, 'You may freely eat of every tree of the garden'" (Genesis 1:29; 2:16).

Indeed, there is a certainty—affirmed in the splendid hymn of creation that is Psalm 104—that "thou dost cause the grass to grow for the cattle, and plants for man to cultivate, that he may bring forth food from the earth, and wine to gladden the heart of man, oil to make his face shine, and bread to strengthen man's heart."

To this original vegetarian diet, after the great flood, God grants humanity meat as well: "The fear of you and the dread of you shall be upon every beast of the earth, and upon every bird of the air, upon everything that creeps on the ground and all the fish of the sea; into your hand they are delivered. Every moving thing that lives shall be food for you; and as I gave you the green plants, I give you everything. Only you shall not eat flesh with its life, that is, its blood" (Genesis 9:2-4). For this reason, "these all look to thee, to give them their food in due season. When thou givest to them, they gather it up; when thou openest thy hand, they are filled with good things" (Psalm 104:27-28). However, when this principle of the universal availability of the good comes to be violated by humankind's sinful egotism, as Nicholas de Chamfort writes in eighteenth-century France, "Society is divided into two classes: those who have more food than hunger, and those with more hunger than food."

Thus, we hear the Biblical admonition to "share your bread with the hungry" (Isaiah 58:7); we are challenged as to whether Lazarus the beggar should be content with just the crumbs that fall from the rich man's table (Luke 16:19-31); we are struck by the denunciation of wasteful luxury and unrestrained consumerism by the prophet Amos (4:1; 6:4-6). In his well-known book *The Prophet*, Lebanese writer Khalil Gibran reminds us, "You should never eat beyond your appetite. Half of your bread belongs to another person and you should set a piece aside for an unexpected guest." Eastern wisdom exhorts us to go further and to set aside two loaves for the poor, one to relieve their hunger and the other to sell so as to buy them flowers, since they, too, have a right to beauty in their lives. For, as we are told by both Deuteronomy and by Jesus, one does not live by bread alone (Deuteronomy 8:3; Matthew 4:4).

For all the foregoing reasons, I would like to reflect here in greater depth on the essential importance of food through various thematic prisms, in three parts. First, I will be drawing our attention to certain basic components of what we eat—bread, wine, water—not simply from a nutritional point of view but rather to discuss their symbolic and existential import. I will then, second, make some space to consider the negation of food by way of two antithetical modalities: one positive—intentional fasting, characteristic of many cultures and not just religions—and one negative—the degenerate use of food in the form of gluttony, one of the so-called seven deadly sins. And in conclusion I will present a short glossary of Biblical terms related to food that takes both its material and symbolic aspects into account.

Der Mensch ist was er isst: this expression, with all of its assonance in its original German, was written by philosopher Ludwig Feuerbach in the journal *Blätter für literarische Unterhaltung* of November 12, 1850, and would soon become the banner for materialism. However, this particular truth, that "man is what he eats," also lends itself to another interpretation of the general nature of our existence, for food in all cultures has also been a symbol of communion in joy (think of Jesus's wedding banquet parables), in pain (as in that particularly Biblical turn of phrase, "to eat the bread of sorrow," such that funeral meals are even today part of the practice of many countries and cultures), and in hospitality (of which we find a delightful example in the story in Genesis 18 where Abraham welcomes the three unknown visitors). French magistrate Anthelme Brillat-Savarin was correct when he observed in his *Physiology of Taste* (1825) that "animals feed, man eats, the man of spirit dines."

As we proceed down this road of religious symbolism in relation to food, we will find, practically speaking, that indeed we come upon an entire panorama of metaphor: there is the paschal banquet of Exodus and the liturgical "communion sacrifice" of the burnt flesh in the Temple. There is the messianic and eschatological banquet, a sign of fulfillment and joy. There is the ethical teaching inherent in Wisdom's banquet (Proverbs 9) and the eucharistic Last Supper of Christ, not to mention the moral character of the very meal with which the Bible itself opens, the very image of the fruit "good for food . . . a delight to the eyes . . . to be desired," from the tree of the knowledge of good and evil (Genesis 3:6). For now, though, we shall simply place before us on our table three very simple foods: bread, wine, and water. Paul Claudel in his *Annunciation of Marie* writes, "Ask the ancient earth and it will answer you with bread and wine." These are the archetypes of nourishment, such that the Hebrew word *leḥem*, "bread," has the same root as the word for "war," precisely because both concern the struggle for life over death.

Naturally, this book has a particularly Christian flavor to it. For example, we notice first how meals have a curious prominence in the story of the life of Jesus. He often sits at table without much care as to who has invited him to do so: sometimes it is a Pharisee who has him as his guest; other times it is a tax collector like Zacchaeus or Matthew. At one point, it is whispered about him that "this man receives sinners and eats with them" (Luke 15:2). In addition, Jesus likes to use the symbol of the banquet, particularly the wedding banquet, to speak of the kingdom of God: here one recalls the parable of the wedding guests (Matthew 22:1-14) or that of the wise and foolish virgins (Matthew 25:1-13). His behavior is such that eventually they say of Jesus, "Behold, a glutton and a drunkard, a friend of tax collectors and sinners!" in contrast to the ascetic practice of John the Baptist, who "has come eating no bread and drinking no wine" (Luke 7:33-34).

In Christian tradition, the two prime works of corporal mercy are to "give food to those who hunger and drink to those who thirst," and for these, two scenes from the Bible remain emblematic. The first is when God—like the father of a family—concerns himself with providing food and water for his people wandering through the desert (water from the rock, manna, and quails). The other is when Jesus provides a lavish feast of loaves and fishes for the crowd that is following him, miraculously multiplying the little bit of food that everyone had on hand.

I

BREAD, WINE, WATER

Leavened and Unleavened Bread

"The kingdom of heaven is like leaven which a woman took and hid in three measures of flour, till it was all leavened" (Matthew 13:33). Jesus takes this image of a mother's everyday task and transforms it into a metaphor for the shattering force of God's kingdom. Beneath it, though, is the primary reality, bread, which we will now briefly consider: in the New Testament alone, the Greek word *artos*, "bread," occurs almost 100 times (97 to be exact). In the *Our Father*, it is clearly invoked as the means by which all life is sustained: "Give us today our daily bread" (Matthew 6:11; cf. Luke 11:3).

The Jesuit Charles Pierre, author of various works of spirituality, states, "Bread possesses a majesty that is almost divine. Eating it slothfully is parasitic. Keeping it carefully is a duty. Refusing to share it is cruelty." Now, in the Bible, bread stands for food in general, such that "partaking of bread" is an expression that simply means to "feed oneself." In the Near East, bread is never given to animals; if one comes upon a piece of bread that has fallen on the ground, one gathers it up and dusts it off. Even today, Arabs do not use a knife to cut bread so as not to "kill" it, since it is considered a living thing. Bread for the poor was made of barley, a rare and highly prized cereal grain. Flour was obtained by way of rudimentary grinding between two stones, one flat, the other upright and turning. Pasta was made in a wooden chest: an Egyptian painting shows bread makers kneading flour with water, salt, and yeast with their feet!

It bears noting, however, that everyday bread of that time was without yeast, that is, a sort of unleavened flatbread, easily made in the desert without an oven (one needed only a flat sheet of stone or metal heated to the right temperature). Nonetheless, Jesus endowed bread with the highest spiritual significance—one cannot help but think of the Eucharist, above all, in this regard, which in the language of the New Testament becomes itself described as the "breaking of the bread" (Acts 2:42). In this act is represented the communion of all the faithful with Christ and with one another. And in this quintessentially Christian rite in which the bread becomes the body of Christ given to the faithful, yet another "material" is transfigured into the effective sign of the blood of Christ: wine.

"Drink of it, all of you"

And Jesus took a cup, and when he had given thanks he gave it to them, saying, "Drink of it, all of you; for this is my blood of the covenant, which is poured out for many for the forgiveness of sins. I tell you I shall not drink again of this fruit of the vine until that day when I drink it new with you in my Father's kingdom. (Matthew 26:27-29)

This beverage that Jesus offers to his disciples at the Last Supper along with the bread has, for the Bible, an immediate and realistic significance as a sign of celebration and joy. Psalm 104:15 sings of wine as that which "gladdens men's hearts," and, indeed, the Messianic age is painted in various oenological colors: "On this mountain the LORD of hosts will make for all peoples a feast of fat things, a feast of wine on the lees, of fat things full of marrow, of wine on the lees well refined" (Isaiah 25:6; Amos 9:14).

In the Bible, starting with Noah, wine is a substance of simplicity and spontaneity, with its capacity to generate happiness, love, friendship, celebration, but with certain risks. In this regard, we cite two striking passages. Sirach, the Wisdom writer of the second century BC, writes:

Do not aim to be valiant over wine, for wine has destroyed many. Fire and water prove the temper of steel, so wine tests hearts in the strife of the proud. Wine is like life to men, if you drink it in moderation. What is life to a man who is without wine? It has been created to make men glad. Wine drunk in season and temperately is rejoicing of heart and gladness of soul. Wine drunk to excess is bitterness of soul, with provocation and stumbling. Drunkenness increases the anger of a fool to his injury, reducing his strength and adding wounds.

But Proverbs, instead, presents a lively portrait of intoxication:

Do not look at wine when it is red, when it sparkles in the cup and goes down smoothly. At the last it bites like a serpent, and stings like an adder. Your eyes will see strange things, and your mind utter perverse things. You will be like one who lies down in the midst of the sea, like one who lies on the top of a mast.

19

(The entire passage from Proverbs 23 is worth reading.)

The Christian religion, therefore, does not consist of some vague interior feeling that is inviting us to detach from earthly realities so as to ascend to some mythic, ascetic heights. It is a faith tied to bodies, history, life on earth. A rushed and superficial society that randomly gobbles down its fast food, that pays no attention to waste, that gets annoyed whenever world hunger is mentioned, that rejects hospitality, this society has lost sight not just of the symbolic dimension of food but has likewise lost the spiritual dimension that food can carry. Therefore, it is important to return to the civilized and symbolic value of food. Charles Lamb, the eighteenth/nineteenth-century English writer, may not have been overstating it when he wrote in his *Essays of Elia*: "I am no Quaker at my food. I confess that I am not indifferent to the kinds of it. . . . I hate a man who swallows it, affecting not to know what he is eating. I suspect his taste in higher matters" ("Grace before Meat").

"This is my body"

As we know, bread and wine have a special prominence on the theological level from the perspective of Christian tradition. Simone Weil, an extraordinary French writer with her own unique relationship to Christianity, wrote in her 1942 *Notebooks*, "God resides in nourishment. Lamb. Bread. And in material made from human labor, bread, wine. In his work, the farmer, if he intends to, gives his flesh so that it may become the flesh of Christ." Thus, we open ourselves to taking in this vision of bread made flesh and wine made blood.

The scene is on everyone's mind. Night is descending on Jerusalem in the first few days of April, in the year AD 30. Jesus goes to an upper room in one of the city's buildings, in a "large room furnished with rugs" that serve as "places to recline," at the low dining table where the evening meal is being prepared in observance of the Hebrew Passover (regardless of the subsequent complex calendar calculations that will try to ascertain the true date of this Jewish

feast day). In any case, the Synoptic Gospels—
Matthew, Mark, and Luke—speak of "the day
of Unleavened Bread, on which the Passover
lamb had to be sacrificed."

The words that Christ says over the bread
and wine, however, go beyond the rite of the
Passover lamb, that observance of nomadic ori-
gin tied to transhumance—the seasonal move-
ment of the flocks for summer grazing—which
became transformed into the feast of Israel's
liberation from slavery in Egypt. Before the
unleavened bread of Jewish ritual, Jesus declares,
"This is my body given for you." Before one of
the four ritual cups of wine, he states, "This is
my blood of the covenant, which is poured out
for many, for the forgiveness of sins" (Mark
14:24; Matthew 26:28). Luke and then later
Paul, on the other hand, will make reference
not so much to the covenant on Mt. Sinai from
Exodus 24, as do Mark and Matthew, but to a
"new covenant" of the Holy Spirit, sung of by
Jeremiah 31:31-34, "This cup is the new covenant of my blood which is poured out for you"
(Luke 22:20; 1 Corinthians 11:25).

Jesus's words emphasize the sacrificial aspect of his act, which the Letter to the Hebrews will use in its own reflections on the death and resurrection of Christ. "He has appeared once for all at the end of the age to put away sin by the sacrifice of himself" (Hebrews 9:26). In fact, the "body" of the Eucharist "is given for you" and the "blood is poured out for many," which in the ancient idiom in fact means "for all." There is still yet another aspect to underscore: the Eucharist—a Greek term that means "act of grace" or "thanksgiving" and which will come to be the term taken up by the tradition to name this sacrificial Paschal rite in Christianity—also itself establishes a covenant, a communion between Christ and the Church and the faithful.

This aspect of the ritual is what becomes driven home in the discourse that John places in the mouth of Jesus in the synagogue at Capernaum after the miracle of the loaves and fishes (John 6:26-58). At that time, Christ's word are placed within the framework of what is virtually a homily preached on the theme of the "bread of life," an image intended, first and foremost, to evoke faith in the person of Christ who gives himself up fully on behalf of the faithful. In this passage, he speaks of his "flesh and blood," using a Semitic expression that refers to the basic reality and identity of a person. Thus, an effective interpersonal communion between God and humanity becomes established, such that those who believe participate in the life of the Divine: "he who eats my flesh and drinks my blood has eternal life, and I will raise him up at the last day" (John 6:51, 54).

Paul goes even further, and in this communion, *koinōnia* in Greek, with the body and blood of Christ in the Eucharist we experience the dawning of our communion-*koinōnia* in fellowship with all believers: "The bread which we break, is it not a participation in the body of Christ? Because there is one bread, we who are many are one body, for we all partake of the one bread" (1 Corinthians 10:16-17; also 11:17-34, where the connection between the Eucharist and brotherly love is reinforced). It is no coincidence, therefore, that the Eucharist, "the breaking of bread," becomes intimately connected to the *koinōnia,* or fellowship, depicted by Luke with regard to the Church in Jerusalem (Acts 2:42).

"All who are thirsty, come to the water!"

After the bread and the wine, we now come to the third component of our "alimentary" symbolic trilogy, water. It has become practically a cliché these days to say that, after the wars fought over oil in the past century, the wars of our present century will be fought over water. And yet, this may not be too far off the mark, as there is a very real risk that this substance that represents life and peace may well be transformed by humans into a symbol of life and death, like oil was. The very aptly named essay entitled *The Water Wars,* by Indian scientist and economist Vandana Shiva (Feltrinelli, 2003), begins with a few lines from the ancient poem of the *Rig-Veda,* one of Hinduism's most sacred texts, composed of 1,028 songs, divided into ten books, dating back to between 1500 and 1000 BC: "Water, it is you who gives us the force of life. Help us to find nourishment so that we may be touched by joy. Let us partake of the supreme delight of your vital fluid, as an affectionate mother, and thus, may we go, sent toward the house of Him for whom your waters give us life and bring us into this world."

As Westerners, though, our own minds may well more easily go to the powerful and basic celebration of water that St. Francis sings of in his *Cantico delle creature*, using four distinct, intense, and limpid adjectives: "Praise you, Lord, for Sister Water, who is most useful and humble and precious and pure." Here, however, with regard to this great symbol of life, we turn simply and humbly to the "great codex" of Western culture, Holy Scripture.

A sun-drenched panorama, an arid plain, a lush green oasis nestled in a valley, a pathway through lonely places, an occasional tree or shrub: this familiar Middle Eastern landscape we may now take for granted, but it is indeed the habitat within which Biblical peoples lived; and so it is, both then and now, that water is the focus of desire and conflict, the archetypal symbol for nomads and settlers alike. The word *mayîm*, "water," appears over 580 times in the Old Testament, just as its Greek equivalent, *hydor*, appears around 80 times in the New (half of which alone are in the Gospel of John). Around 1,500 verses of the Old Testament might be described as "soaked" with water, since, above and beyond even those explicit uses of the word, there is indeed a whole constellation of thematic realities that revolve about this most precious of all elements, ranging from the perilous *yam*, "the sea," to the calm river Jordan, on to and including all the various kinds of rain (each of which has a different Hebrew name according to its season—autumnal, winter, and springtime), rivers, torrents, channels, springs, wells, cisterns, heavenly reservoirs, the flood, the ocean, and so forth. And that is not even addressing verbs connected with water, such as drinking, watering, thirsting, drying, pouring, immersing (i.e., "baptizing," in New Testament Greek), washing, purifying. . . .

This stream of water runs straight through all of Holy Scripture, giving witness to an ancient thirst that is tied to a geographical and ecological place characterized by dryness. It is not by chance that the Bible opens with the creation of light and water (Genesis 1:3-10), with the coming of the rain and the rising up of the streams (Genesis 2:4-6), and then comes to a conclusion with "the river of the water of life, as clear as crystal, flowing from the throne of God and of the Lamb" (Revelation 22:1). In between, of course, there is always a thirst, always an anxious search for water. One need only bring to mind the cry of the Israelites in the desert, "Give us water to drink!" (Exodus 17:2) or the drought held as a divine curse pronounced by the prophet in the name of God: "Now Elijah the Tishbite, from Tishbe in Gilead, said to Ahab, 'As the LORD, the God of Israel, lives, whom I serve, there will be neither dew nor rain in the next few years except at my word'" (1 Kings 17:1).

Jeremiah has left us one of the most vivid and dramatic portraits of this endemic scourge of the Near East:

The nobles send their servants for water;
    they go to the cisterns
    but find no water.
They return with their jars unfilled;
    dismayed and despairing,
    they cover their heads.
The ground is cracked
    because there is no rain in the land;
the farmers are dismayed
    and cover their heads.
Even the doe in the field
    deserts her newborn fawn
    because there is no grass.
Wild donkeys stand on the barren heights
    and pant like jackals;
their eyes fail
    for lack of food.
                (Jeremiah 14:3-6)

Thus, when clouds gather and the rains come, the people are convinced that they have received God's blessing, as in Deuteronomy: "The LORD will open the heavens, the storehouse of his bounty, to send rain on your land in season and to bless all the work of your hands. You will lend to many nations but will borrow from none" (Deuteronomy 28:12). Over all, the Creator and Father of all peoples cares for each one of his creatures regardless of merit, as Jesus will say, "He causes his sun to rise on the evil and the good, and sends rain on the righteous and the unrighteous" (Matthew 5:45). When spring arrives with its rains, the psalmist—in a poetic set of images of extraordinary resonance—envisions the Lord passing over the earth with his water cart:

> You drench its furrows and level its ridges;
>   you soften it with showers and bless its
>   crops.
> You crown the year with your bounty,
>   and your carts overflow with abundance.
> The grasslands of the wilderness overflow;
>   the hills are clothed with gladness.
> The meadows are covered with flocks
>   and the valleys are mantled with grain;
>   they shout for joy and sing.
>   (Psalm 65:10-14)

And in the book of Isaiah, the Lord calls to humanity using the word of the water carrier who would go about the village streets of the Near East, "All you who thirst, come to the water!" (Isaiah 55:1).

Water as Symbol

Irrigation and hydraulic technology represent our human contribution to this Biblical theme: one need only visit the fortress of Megiddo in Galilee with its imposing aqueduct or follow the 540-meter-long tunnel dug in the eighth century BC under King Hezekiah to bring water from the spring of Gihon to the reservoir of Siloe in Jerusalem. (A carved stone, now in the archeological museum of Istanbul, memorializes the thrilling moment when the last bit of excavation was cleared and the two teams of workers, digging from opposite sides, at last met in the middle.)

Precisely because our physical life depends upon it, water becomes a symbol of absolute value and thus of our spiritual life as well, our transcendence. Melville, in his "water novel" *Moby Dick*, writes,

Why did the old Persians hold the sea holy? Why did the Greeks give it a separate deity, and own brother of Jove? Surely all this is not without meaning. And still deeper the meaning of that story of Narcissus, who because he could not grasp the torment-ing, mild image he saw in the fountain, plunged into it and was drowned. But that same image, we ourselves see in all rivers and oceans. It is the image of the ungrasp-able phantom of life; and this is the key to it all. (Chapter 1)

The Bible approaches water in a similar key and through a prism of various meanings, not all of which are positive. We need only to think of the flood, sent as a sign and as an act of divine punishment, or again of the exodus and the crossing of the Red Sea, which became the tomb of the Egyptians, or as mentioned above, the *yam* or sea, which deserves its own fuller symbolic exploration, serving for Israel as an image of chaos, of nothingness, and even of evil: thus, Christ walks upon the water, and elsewhere sends those unclean animals, the pigs, into the sea, and yet again succeeds in holding his terrified disciple Peter above the water (Matthew 14:24-31).

Water, however, is first of all and above all a sign of life and transcendence. So it is enough to list here just some of the many metaphoric meanings that water carries: it is never merely sweetly contemplated in the Bible as "clear fresh sweet water," as in Petrarch, but rather celebrated as a reminder of higher, hidden realities. Water, in this way, becomes a symbol of God par excellence, the source of all life, as in Jeremiah's unforgettable image: "They have forsaken me, the spring of living water, and have dug their own cisterns, broken cisterns that cannot hold water" (Jeremiah 2:13).

Water is a sign of God's word, without which one suffocates and dries out: "'The days are coming,' declares the Sovereign LORD, 'when I will send a famine through the land—not a famine of food or a thirst for water, but a famine of hearing the words of the LORD'" (Amos 8:11); or "As the rain and the snow come down from heaven, and do not return to it without watering the earth and making it bud and flourish, so that it yields seed for the sower and bread for the eater, so is my word that goes out from my mouth" (Isaiah 55:10-11).

Water is a symbol of God's wisdom that flows to and through Israel.

> The Law overflows with Wisdom like the Pishon River, like the Tigris at fruit-picking time. The Law brims over with understanding like the Euphrates, like the Jordan at harvest time. It sparkles with teachings like the Nile, like the Gihon at grape-picking time. . . . As for me, I thought of myself as an irrigation canal bringing water from a river into a garden. I only intended to water my orchard and flower beds, but the canal soon became a river, and the river became a sea. (Sirach 24:25-27, 30-31)

Water announces the Messianic age and the rebirth of humanity: "Then will the lame leap like a deer, and the mute tongue shout for joy. Water will gush forth in the wilderness and streams in the desert. The burning sand will become a pool, the thirsty ground bubbling springs" (Isaiah 35:6-7).

Indeed, water becomes an emblem of Christ, as is implied in the well-known conversation he has with the Samaritan woman at the well. "Whoever drinks the water I give them will never thirst. Indeed, the water I give them will become in them a spring of water welling up to eternal life" (John 4:14). For this reason, the Gospel writer insists that from the pierced side of the crucified Christ there appeared "a sudden flow of blood and water" (John 19:34). As Jesus implies in his words to the Samaritan woman, water becomes a sign of the new life, infused with the Holy Spirit of those who believe. During Succoth, the Jewish festival of booths (which itself involves a ritual using the waters of Siloe), Jesus proclaims, "Let anyone who is thirsty come to me and drink. Whoever believes in me, as Scripture has said, rivers of living water will flow from within them.' By this he meant the Spirit, whom those who believed in him were later to receive" (John 7:37-39).

Water, therefore, then becomes an image of the new life of the faithful with which is purified one's sinful heart ("Wash me of all my sins," Psalm 51:4), according to a cleansing rite common to nearly all religious cultures. It represents an inward regeneration that will bring forth the fruits of righteousness: "That person is like a tree planted by streams of water, which yields its fruit in season and whose leaf does not wither—whatever they do prospers" (Psalm 1:3).

But above all, water is always the supreme symbol of that God for whom human beings always thirst, and this is the constant prayer of all who seek God with a sincere heart. "As the deer pants for streams of water, so my soul pants for you, my God. My soul thirsts for God, for the living God. When can I go and meet with God?... You, God, are my God, earnestly I seek you; I thirst for you, my whole being longs for you, in a dry and parched land where there is no water" (Psalm 42:1; 63:1).

"I was hungry and you gave me to eat"

Bread, wine, water: these are signs of survival through food, as well as emblems of spirituality and faith. In concluding our discussion here, I would like to focus on a theme especially dear to the Bible, that of hospitality. This moral obligation engages every faithful person who, from the midst of a hungry crowd, hears the call to be welcomed at the world's table, where a chosen few hoard immense quantities of wealth in an appearance of unrestrained, dissipated opulence. In the biography of Socrates that Diogenes Laertius has left us in *Lives of the Philosophers* (first century BC), the famous Greek figure states that while "many men live to eat, he rather ate to live." In a consumer society, therefore, it is important to uphold that spirit of generosity that is expressed in a hospitable welcome to the immense crowd of those who hunger.

37

The scene narrated in Genesis 18 is quite vivid. Everything is motionless in the summer heat, but, just as three visitors appear on the horizon, nearly frenetic activity suddenly ensues: Abraham runs to meet them, orders that water be brought to wash the feet of these travelers; he rushes to get them food, hurried by his wife, Sarah, slaughters a calf himself for dinner, and, as his guests dine, he stands by them, ready to serve. In the ancient Near East, hospitality was not just a sacred duty but was organized into strict norms of behavior.

For this reason, betraying a guest was considered a very grave crime, evidence for which follows immediately upon the story just told, when these three visitors come to Lot's house in Sodom and run the risk of being subjected to violence (Genesis 19, as well as the terrible story found in Judges 19). A stranger welcomed as a guest enjoyed the same rights as a resident, as is expressed by this Biblical injunction: "When a foreigner resides among you in your land, do not mistreat them. The foreigner residing among you must be treated as your native-born.

Love them as yourself, for you were foreigners in Egypt. I am the LORD your God" (Leviticus 19:33-34).

As we have already seen, Jesus in his itinerant ministry of preaching, accepted offers of hospitality with joy, sometimes sitting at table within what was considered a questionable social context (for example, with tax collectors Matthew and Zacchaeus or with people of ill repute). And he suggested to his disciples that they do likewise. "Whenever you enter a house, stay there until you leave that town" (Mark 6:10). God will reward even the simple gesture of offering a cup of water (Matthew 10:42). And it is precisely along these lines that Jesus loves the tender and thoughtful hospitality shown him by Mary, Martha, and Lazarus (Luke 10:38-42; John 12:1-11).

In the New Testament the practice of fraternal hospitality shown to members of the various church communities has a prominent place, and Paul himself, during his missionary journeys, is a guest of various families (see, for example, Romans 16:23). In fact, his last letter, addressed to his friend Philemon, is sealed with a request: "And one thing more: Prepare a guest room for me, because I hope to be restored to you in answer to your prayers" (verse 22).

In keeping with this value of hospitality that runs through all of Scripture, we are invited to extend a generous welcome ourselves particularly to the least among us and to those who are marginalized, keeping the injunction from the Letter to the Hebrews always firmly in mind: "Do not forget to show hospitality to strangers, for by so doing some people have shown hospitality to angels without knowing it" (Hebrews 13:2). For, as Jesus has said, "Anyone who welcomes you welcomes me, and anyone who welcomes me welcomes the one who sent me" (Matthew 10:40).

II

THE VIRTUE OF FASTING AND THE VICE OF GLUTTONY

"This is the fast the Lord wants"

The topic of fasting is fraught with many complexities. Some fast by necessity because of a lack of food and due to famine, that scourge described in the Apocalypse as the third of the dark horsemen, the black one, which ravages the face of the earth.

> When the Lamb opened the third seal, I heard the third living creature say, "Come!" I looked, and there before me was a black horse! Its rider was holding a pair of scales in his hand. Then I heard what sounded

41

like a voice among the four living creatures, saying, "Two pounds of wheat for a
day's wages, and six pounds of barley for a
day's wages, and do not damage the oil and
the wine!" (Revelation 6:5-6).

This representation of famine, of rationed
food, of exorbitant prices, is strikingly clear and
describes conditions well known throughout
our world.

Then there is politically motivated fasting that has noble aims and often becomes a
weapon of extortion against those in power.
There is, likewise, dieting, an outgrowth of a
culture of wealth and excess, which sometimes
is in turn tied to various psycho-physical disor-
ders such as bulimia or obesity. G. K. Chester-
ton, noted English Catholic writer, is said to
have remarked, "The other day in the under-
ground I had the pleasure of giving my seat up
to three ladies!" And finally, there is the tragic
illness of anorexia, in which a fear of eating can
transform itself easily into a source of death.

However, in contrast to all these other forms of dietary abstinence, there is the religious fast.

Some time ago, a French bishop told me this story. Having been invited to speak at a school as part of a series of presentations on various religions, he began by asking the children a question, "What is Lent?" (since he was speaking, in fact, during this period of liturgical preparation for the central feast of the Christian year, the solemnity of Easter). The native French students murmured among themselves, but there were students from other ethnic backgrounds as well. Finally, one of the French students gathered the courage to say, "It's how Christians observe Ramadan!" This story is emblematic of the socio-cultural evolution of our times: the basic frame of reference, in a dazed and distracted Europe, has become external and extrinsic, such that our understanding of reality no longer derives from autochthonous but rather from allogenous sources. For this reason, I would like to engage in a full consideration of fasting as a religious act.

The word in Romance languages is, of course, of Latin derivation, *jejunus*, which means "hungry." From *jejunus* its opposite in those languages is likewise derived, *disjejunare*, as in the French *déjeuner*, which means literally to "break a fast." In the Gospels, one recalls that, before entering into his public ministry, Jesus "fasted forty days and forty nights" (Matthew 4:2). The Greek verb used here is *nesteuein*, "to fast," which occurs twenty times in the New Testament along with its two derivative nouns, *nesteia* and *nestis*, "fast," which appear five times and two times, respectively. In the other Biblical language, Hebrew, the root word *tzum* is used instead, which as both verb and noun appears forty-seven times in the Old Testament and is used in both Arabic and Ethiopian to specifically denote a religious fast.

"Abba Eulogius told his disciple: My son, little by little, take care to restrict your stomach by way of fasting. For as a wineskin becomes softer as it is stretched, so too does the stomach when it is filled with much food. But if it is given little, it shrinks and needs less and less."

This story from the Desert Fathers illustrates the original rationale behind the ascetic practice of fasting, a universal practice that developed into a religious choice, as exemplified in the Hebrew Yom Kippur, the great day of penitential expiation, which enjoins a complete abstention from food, sexual enjoyment, and work, as well as in the Muslim month of Ramadan, one of the "five pillars" of Islam, and as in the unbroken Christian tradition.

It was stated earlier that modern secularization has often reduced this venerable spiritual act into nothing more than a diet, and yet all the major religious traditions have firmly held that fasting is an act that by its very nature is symbolic, in the most fundamental sense of that term. We need only to recall Isaiah's lapidary, incisive declaration: "Is not this the kind of fasting I have chosen: to loose the chains of injustice and untie the cords of the yoke, to set the oppressed free and break every yoke? Is it not to share your food with the hungry and to provide the poor wanderer with shelter—when you see the naked, to clothe them, and not to turn away from your own flesh and blood?" (Isaiah 58:6-7).

Or we may call to mind Jesus's ironic judgment on the ritualistic abstinence of those who "look somber and disfigure their faces." In contrast to these, he abjures his disciples to "put oil on your head and wash your faces" (Matthew 6:16-17), so that fasting may not be put on display but rather be an expression of an interior intention, self-discipline, freedom from consumption and egotism, from attachments and illusory needs, a purification of the spirit, self-control, transcendence of the senses. The same Desert Fathers did not refrain from noting that "it is better to drink wine humbly and to drink water proudly."

Even in Islam, the voice of one of its great mystical teachers, al-Ghazali (1058–1111), admonishes the faithful that true fasting is to abstain from sins of the tongue and of other body parts so as to free oneself from "all that is not God." Even Hindu tradition, where Gandhi demonstrated the "political" effectiveness of fasting, holds a similar view: "Fasting makes no sense if it does not result in sobriety and if it is not accompanied by a constant desire for self-discipline. Whoever subjugates his senses is the first and most important among men. All the virtues reside in him."

Temperance: The Fourth Cardinal Virtue

As a corollary to the above observations, we might do well to dust off the fourth of the classic "cardinal" virtues, that is, temperance. It is interesting to note that in Christian tradition, this virtue was called *enkrateia*, that is "mastery of self, self-control," as opposed to *sophrōsynē*, "wisdom, moderation," the correct application of thoughts and passions (in the history of ethics, a similar distinction was also made). The correct use of food is, all the same, the most common connotation of temperance, the transgression of which was portrayed quite vividly in Marco Ferreri's 1973 film *La grande bouffe*, which recreated in an especially powerful way Trimalchio's dinner from Petronius's first-century *Satyricon*. Four friends go down a dark path toward killing themselves through an orgy of food and sex, consumed in the course of a sort of "retreat" (certainly not spiritual) in an aged Parisian villa. As portrayed by the actors Ugo Tognazzi, Marcello Mastroianni, Michel Piccoli, and Philippe Noiret, they each die, one after another, choking on meat, desserts, and wine, through a macabre ritual presided over by the "priestess," played by Andréa Ferréol.

So, yes, alimentary temperance is, indeed, sobriety, impulse control, mastery of the senses, and self-respect, but it must also involve the affirmative expression of charity toward others, as the Letter of James admonishes: "Suppose a brother or a sister is without clothes and daily food. If one of you says to them, 'Go in peace; keep warm and well fed,' but does nothing about their physical needs, what good is it? In the same way, faith by itself, if it is not accompanied by action, is dead" (James 2:15-16). This call to moderation is, thus, necessary, as is likewise clear in the charge St. Paul gives to his disciple Titus: "Similarly, encourage the young men to be self-controlled. In everything set them an example by doing what is good" (Titus 2:6-7). But this is simply the first step to be taken inwardly: "Therefore be alert and of sober mind so that you may pray" (1 Peter 4:7). To the personal transcendence represented by sobriety must therefore be added fraternal charity and a focus on spirituality, and it is precisely this implicitly affirmative dimension that makes temperance neither masochism nor a bitter, dark asceticism.

It provides for a balanced life of the individual; it is a sign of serene detachment from material things and shows forth in an interior and behavioral dignity. For this reason, one reads in the *Talmud*, that great collection of Jewish wisdom, that "gluttony has killed more men than hunger has," arising from an awareness of having to deal with a degeneration of morality more than a physiological phenomenon when the virtue of temperance is lost. It is not by chance that early Christianity—before it was strongly influenced subsequently by Neoplatonism—is not especially disdainful of the body or of food, such that Jesus is often portrayed at table to the point of being labeled by his enemies as a "glutton and a drunkard" (Matthew 11:19).

As we briefly explore the various aspects of this virtue, which Paul considered a source of light in the soul, as over against the darkness that overcomes those who get drunk (see 1 Thessalonians 5:5-8), we move forward, by contrast, to consider its opposite, the deadly sin of gluttony. In Carlo Goldoni's 1750 comedy *The Coffee Shop*, the shop owner Rodolfo says, gluttony is "a vice that never ends, a vice that grows and grows as a man gets older and older." It is a vice that continually takes on new and different forms, expressed in ways we are all familiar with—nicotine addiction, drug abuse, alcoholism. For this reason, it is necessary to assert the value of temperance as a moral virtue that regulates two fundamentally human actions, nourishment and procreation (the latter of which would of course encompass a discussion of sexual ethics, which is beyond the focus of this work).

"Gluttony kills more than the sword"

Food in itself, as is often said, is both necessary and good. It is its use, through the exercise of free will, that can turn it into something perverse, making of it an idol and leading to the vice of gluttony, one of the seven deadly sins. Or, as the Latin writer Quintilian (first century) puts it, *non ut edam vivo, sed ut vivam edo* ("I do not live to eat, I eat to live"). Our Western society, even in the late phase of economic recession, has a disordered relationship to food: on the one hand, advertising pushes unbridled consumption, while on the other pushing all forms and manner of dieting for weight loss. As was noted earlier, the psychopathology of bulimia is on par with that of anorexia, both expressions of an illness around food that arises from the wealth of Western culture, proving in some ways the truth of the medieval proverb that "gluttony kills more than the sword": *Mas mató la cena que sanó Avicenna*, "Medicine of Avicenna is less powerful than gastronomy."

Right from the beginning of the Bible, greed for the fruit of the tree of the knowledge of good and evil, the drunkenness of Noah, and the furious hunger of Esau lead to a loss of values. Amos (6:4-6), Isaiah (28:1-3), and Daniel (chapter 6) speak of the palace orgies awash in food and wine and "elegant dinners" that stand for decadence of all sorts and a rejection of morality. Upon these, however, falls divine judgment (as in the clamorous, thrilling scene of Balshazzar's banquet in chapter 5 of Daniel). The contrast between wastefulness and misery is drawn sharply and powerfully in the parable of the "rich man and Lazarus" (Luke 16:19-31), which stands even today as a striking image of the contradiction that still afflicts our society. On the table of good things created by God, a very small and exclusive group of people have before them an enormous accumulation of wealth, which they consume voraciously.

One thinks of Nabal, in the book of Samuel, the low-class land owner married to the beautiful Abigail, and whose name already tips one off as to the agenda of the story, because the word *nabal* in Hebrew means "fool." After an enormous eating and drinking binge, "his heart failed him and he became like a stone. About ten days later, the Lord struck Nabal and he died" (1 Samuel 25:37-38). A fatal stroke, therefore, brings to a conclusion his foolish, pleasure-bent existence. *Gargantua et Pantagruel*, Rabelais' sixteenth-century masterpiece, is an irony-drenched morality tale along the same lines.

On the other side of this table of wealth, however, a huge crowd of Lazaruses press forward, the poor and hungry of every age who beg for crumbs from this table. In this light, thus, we understand the symbolic meaning of the miracle of the multiplication of the loaves as performed by Jesus, the hungry masses finally and fully fed simply through sharing small portions of bread and fish, the leftovers of the table of the wealthy. The true remedy to gluttonous gorging is not pure and simply asceticism, fasting at all cost, but rather the sort of generosity that we see practiced in brotherly *koinōnia*, the sharing of goods and possessions that characterized the early Christian community in Jerusalem (Acts 2:42-47; 4:32-35). And let us not forget that Jesus himself loved to eat at table as a form of encounter with people who were less socially desirable, to the point of being the target of Pharisaical judgment. Detachment from material possessions, from excess, from overeating ought to result in sharing with the Lazaruses of this world without having to deny the ascetic value of fasting as a diet more for the soul than the body, as has already been stated.

The Bible does not lack for stories about one specific form of gluttony, that is, alcohol abuse, which was (and still is) a precursor to and co-occurring disorder with drug addiction. The Wisdom literature of the Bible is full of denunciations of the degeneration represented by those who love wine. A single line of Sirach suffices in this regard: "Bitterness of soul comes of wine drunk to excess out of temper or bravado. Drunkenness excites the stupid to a fury to his own harm, it reduces his strength while leading to blows" (Sirach 31:29-30). And Paul does not hesitate to locate the drunkards among those who "will not inherit the kingdom of God" (1 Corinthians 6:10).

The sin of gluttony is forcefully condemned by Dante in the third of the nine circles of Hell and in the sixth of the seventh terraces of the mountain of Purgatory. On the latter, gluttons move forward beneath trees heavy with unreachable fruit toward which these sinners stretch out their hands "like little children eager and deluded/Who pray, and he they pray to doth not answer" (*Purgatory* XXIV:108-109). Austrian writer Karl Kraus stated that "vice and virtue are related to one another, like coal and diamonds," which share the common element of carbon. In other words, it is a person's free choice that in due course degrades God's creation since, as the Book of Wisdom states, "For he fashioned all things that they might have being, and the creatures of the world are wholesome; there is not a destructive drug among them" (1:14).

Before vice, therefore, almost like the back side of a medal, there is virtue, that is, the positive aspect of food: eating is fundamental to our survival, and moderation is a virtue that does not limit; indeed, it actually acts to enhance the joy of a festive meal of, say, a family brought together around the table, as sung in Psalm 128. For this reason, we would do well to bring ourselves back to the beauty of the table, often spoiled by the frenzy of modern life, which contents itself with nourishment by way of fast food, gobbling down things to eat. Important occasions, like births, baptisms, weddings, reunions, even funerals, are always punctuated by sharing a meal with friends and family, such as was described by the Jewish Biblical ritual known as a "communion sacrifice," a holy meal.

Jesus's most significant warning to us about the nature of created things, in particular what we eat, shifts the accent from the definition of vice to the conscience of the person:

"Don't you see that nothing that enters a person from the outside can defile them? For it doesn't go into their heart but into

their stomach, and then out of the body."
(In saying this, Jesus declared all foods
clean.) He went on, "What comes out of a
person is what defiles them. For it is from
within, out of a person's heart, that evil
thoughts come.... All these evils come
from inside and defile a person." (Mark
7:18-23)

III

A SMALL GLOSSARY OF FOOD

Here I would like to present, in a very brief way, a small Biblical glossary in which the Biblical and everyday categories of food-related terms are presented along with their theological and cultural meanings in light of the reality of the Incarnation, which transforms Biblical thought into a religion of the body and not just a vague ethereal ritualism.

DRINK: This general term refers to the act of drinking from a spring or a well. In the First Letter to the Corinthians (12:13), however, the phrase "we were all given one Spirit to drink" occurs, and before that, from the same section of this letter, being "baptized by one Spirit" is described, so that many believe Paul is speaking of the gift of the Holy Spirit given in the sacrament of Confirmation, whereas others believe he was referring to the Eucharist (see 1 Corinthians 10:4).

VINEGAR: In reality, this term refers also to a light, tart wine that was commonly drunk among the poor. The offer of vinegar to Jesus on the cross is presented as an act of compassion so as to alleviate his thirst in the Gospel of Matthew (27:48), but it is seen as an act of derision in Luke (23:26) and in John (19:28), who allude to Psalm 69:22 in which "poison and vinegar" are given to the righteous man by his enemies.

LAMB: This common animal within the pastoral landscape of Biblical times came to take on—as did the role of pastor, as well—deep symbolic meaning. Thus, it became the Passover sacrifice, slain and consumed (Exodus 12), which then in turn became the symbol of the messianic Suffering Servant of the Lord (Isaiah

53:7) and then of Christ crucified (John 19:36). Jesus comes to be called, by John the Baptist, "the Lamb of God who takes away the sin of the world" (John 1:29), and the glorified Christ is often sung, in Revelation, as "the Lamb, who was slain, to receive power and wealth and wisdom and strength and honor and glory and praise!" (Revelation 5:12).

TREE OF THE KNOWLEDGE OF GOOD AND EVIL: "And the LORD God commanded the man, 'You are free to eat from any tree in the garden; but you must not eat from the tree of the knowledge of good and evil, for when you eat from it you will certainly die'" (Genesis 2:16-17). It is obvious that this tree is not a botanical plant but rather a moral symbol. This "knowledge" in the Bible is the comprehensive human experience of intellect, will, emotions, and actions. "Good and evil" are the two poles of morality. "To eat" is to take part in this experience of one's own free will, disregarding the morality established by God and creating instead one's own morality, personal and subjective, which is what man and woman decide to do with their freedom (Genesis 3:1-7).

TREE OF LIFE: This symbol is important in the ancient Near East, representing a divine immortality denied to human beings, as presented in the fascinating Mesopotamian poem *The Epic of Gilgamesh*, in which the hero vainly believes he can lay claim to this tree of eternal youth. The image also makes a brief appearance in the Biblical story of "earthly paradise" but serves only a secondary function (Genesis 2:9 and 3:22), as well as in Revelation (2:7): its fruits are signs of an eternal and glorious communion of the righteous with God.

CHALICE: Although a liturgical vessel (both in the Jewish rite of Passover as well as in the Eucharist), the chalice also acquires the symbolic meaning of a person's fate, based on the idea that a cup contains only a limited amount of liquid. Thus, we read of the cup of salvation (Psalm 111:13), but also, in reference to divine judgment, the cup of the Lord's wrath, and as a symbol of death, as in Jesus's words in the Garden of Gethsemane (Mark 14:36).

FLESH: The Biblical term above all has the general anthropological meaning of humans as creatures, fragile, limited, and mortal, which then becomes a theological category, as when John describes God's incarnation in Christ as "the Word became flesh" (John 1:14). In Paul, however, the term takes on a negative connotation as the source of human sin, while the flesh of all animals is given by God to human beings to eat after the flood, superceding the vegetarian diet originally established at the beginning of creation (Genesis 1:29-30).

OVEN: Two types of oven were in use at that time: an oven for bread, built on the ground and open on top, heated with burning coals so as to bake flatbread, and a kiln for ceramic ware, built with two levels, with space for clay objects to be fired on the upper level. The oven's burning fire becomes in the Bible a symbol of God's effective presence (Genesis 15:17) and of his judgment upon evil (Malachi 3:2).

BREAKING OF BREAD: This expression is a translation of the Greek *klasis tou artou* and was well known in the Jewish world (Lamentations 4:4). In Christianity, however, it becomes an allusion to the Eucharist, a specific sacrament of the Church. "To break bread" originally indicated a sign of fellowship in the course of a communal meal, but for Christians, it takes on a new and sacred dimension while still retaining its original meaning of fellowship.

MILK AND HONEY: Together, these are the two foods of nomadic people and as such therefore represent well-being when found in abundance. Thus, the Promised Land is described in Scripture as a land flowing with milk and honey (Deuteronomy 6:3, for example). Some, however, think that this expression may refer to a specific kind of nomadic dish.

YEAST: This fermenting agent has two symbolic meanings. The first is as a symbol of power, since it makes the dough rise (Matthew 13:33). The other is as a symbol of impurity, so that Passover bread must be "unleavened," that is, free of yeast. In this sense, for example, Paul speaks of the "old bread leavened with malice and wickedness" (1 Corinthians 5:8).

LOCUSTS: The scourge of Eastern agriculture, this insect—which has more than one word for its name in Hebrew, according to its species—was also edible, as attested to by John the Baptist, who "fed on locusts and wild honey" (Matthew 3:4), and by other ancient Mesopotamian texts with recipes based on locusts and grasshoppers.

MILLING: Women (Ecclesiastes 12:4) were the ones who milled the grain to make flour using a cylindrical millstone that rolled horizontally, as has been illustrated in various archeological finds and in ancient Egyptian paintings. Later mills from Hellenistic and Roman times would be more complex, turned by animals such as donkeys (Matthew 18:6). As a symbol of daily women's work, mills are also sometimes signs of God's sudden appearance: "Two women will be grinding with a hand mill; one will be taken and the other left" (Matthew 24:41).

To Eat: We know that the frequency of a word's appearance indicates the importance of what it signifies to a culture. For this reason, we must acknowledge the plethora of words used for "eating" in the two Biblical languages, Hebrew and Greek. In Hebrew, we have *'akal*, "to eat, to consume"; *ta'am*, "to taste or savor"; *saba'*, "to eat one's fill"; *barâ*, "to consume"; *leḥem*, "bread, food." In Greek, however, the foremost term used is *esthiō*, "to eat," to which are associated the following words having the same meaning with different shadings, *trogō*, *bibrōskō*, *metechō*. And then, there are *trephō*, "to nourish or feed," *aristaō* and *deipneō*, "to feast," *geuomai*, "to taste or savor." Other derivations are *brōsis* and *brōma*, "food" (from *bibrōskō*). Obviously also important is *artos*, "bread," as well as *psomion*, the "morsel" Jesus offers Judas at the Last Supper (John 13:26-27).

Manna: The word describes a resinous substance that is found on a particular tamerind bush in the Sinai (*tamerix mannifera*) following insect damage to the bark. The Bedouins considered it edible. In the Bible—explained popularly as having gotten its name from the Hebrew *man hû?*, "what is it?"—it is a sign of the fatherly care of God who feeds his people in the desert (Exodus 16:15). John uses it as a symbol for the Eucharist (6:31-33, 58).

HARVEST: This important and festive action in the life of a farming people is often used in the Bible as a symbol of the last judgment: just as the wheat will be separated from the chaff, so, too, will the good be separated from the evil (Matthew 13:24-30, 37-43). In Revelation, the angel of divine judgment holds in his hand a sickle with which the field of the world will be harvested (14:15-16).

OIL: Along with its normal meaning of a liquid drawn from olives, this Biblical term also refers to perfumes and fragrances used in cosmetics and in funeral rites. Hence, the connotation of the sinful woman's gesture, as told in Luke

(7:37-38), and of Mary, sister of Lazarus, as told in John (12:1-8). A particular balsamic oil was used—as is still the case within Christian liturgies—for priestly or regal consecrations (see, for example, Psalm 133 and 1 Samuel 1:1; 16:13).

SHEEP: As the basic unit of a flock, sheep thus become—in Biblical pastoral symbolism—an image of the faithful follower of Christ the Good Shepherd. In the appearance of the Risen Christ alongside the Sea of Galilee, John uses two different Greek words to indicate Peter's mission: feed my *arnia*, that is, baby lambs, and feed my *probata*, that is, adult sheep, perhaps in order to emphasize the variety of God's people.

FISH: These have a special place among the animals of the Bible, particularly within the Gospels, primarily due to the fact that the first disciples of Jesus were fishermen on the Sea of Galilee. The Old Testament classified various fish according to their features as edible or not according to ritual dietary laws. The Greek word *ichthus* became, within early Christian iconography, a "fish" that symbolized Christ, because it was made up of the first letters of the phrase *Iesous Christos, Theou Huios Sōtēr*, "Jesus Christ, Son of God, Savior."

PIG: This animal was considered ritually unclean and thus inedible, for reasons both enviromental-climatic as well as in folk tradition (Leviticus 11:7). During the Maccabean revolt (second century BC), against Syro-Hellenistic rule, a Jew, Eleazar, would rather be killed than to violate the proscription against eating pig, which then comes to represent all Jewish tradition (2 Maccabees 6:18-31). In the parable of the Prodigal Son, his misfortune is represented by his being sent out to the fields to feed the pigs.

CLEANLINESS: In all religions there is a line between what is sacred and what is profane. To go from the latter to the former, therefore, a ritual purification is necessary that entails not just washing but ritual regulations of various sorts.

Among these, some pertain to food, according to ancient folk traditions. For example, "clean" animals are ruminants and those with cloven hooves, as well as fish with scales (see the parable of the net, in Matthew 13:47-48). These constitute the rules for keeping *kosher*, which means "fitting," in order to maintain ritual purity, still used today among Jews (see Leviticus 11; Deuteronomy 14:3-21; and 2 Maccabees 6–7). Christ is critical of these proscriptions, emphasizing instead interior, moral purity (Mark 7:14-23; cf. Acts 10:9-20; 11:1-18; 15:7-11).

SACRIFICE: In all religions, sacrifice is a fundamental component of ritual action, despite a diversity of forms. The animal victim or plant offering embodies the faithful, who offer themselves to the divinity in order to establish a bond of communion. In the Old Testament, there is a varied gamut of sacrifices, the liturgical celebrations of which are all meticulously described. The most solemn of these is the "holocaust," which, as the Greek word suggests, presupposed the complete consumption by fire of the victim, which thereby ascends to God (in Hebrew, the rite is termed 'olah, "that which goes up" to God, who "smells the pleasing fragrance of it" (Genesis 8:21), that is, accepts it with favor. Another important sacrificial rite was termed "communion" and was comprised of a sacred meal: the greater part of the offering was burned, part of which was then set aside for the priests (and by implication, for God), while the rest was consumed by the faithful within the temple. Through this sacred banquet, in which God was ideally participating, a bond of communion and intimacy was established with the divine.

BLOOD: It was forbidden to drink or touch blood because it was a sign of life. Jesus upset those who heard him offer his blood as drink, even though he was referring to the mystical communion of the Eucharist (John 6:55-56). "Flesh and blood" is an expression indicating the reality of human mortality.

EGG: In the Bible, we read of the nest with birds' eggs (Deuteronomy 22:6), the egg forgotten in the sand by the ostrich (Job 39:12), and eggs hatched by the partridge (Jeremiah 17:11). Jesus, instead, compares eggs with the tiny white Palestinian scorpion that looks like a small egg when it rolls up into a ball between the rocks in the desert, and he uses this image to bring forward the fatherly love of God who will not give us poison but instead will feed us with healthy food.

VINE: This component of Palestinian farming became a symbol of Israel with the prophet Hosea, who compared the people of Israel to a "spreading vine." The well-known "song of the vine" is in Isaiah, who decries Israel's faithlessness. Equally well known is Jesus's parable of the murderous vineyard tenants (Matthew 21:33-46). As vineyards are cultivated throughout the Mediterranean region, wine becomes a meaningful presence on the table of the Jewish people, as mentioned earlier, and is celebrated as a source of joy and accompaniment to festivities (Psalm 104:15; John 2:12), as well as a Messianic symbol (Isaiah 25:6). Excessive consumption of wine, however, is vigorously and harshly labeled a vice (Proverbs 23:29-35).

TARES: The original Greek word was a plural noun that indicated a plant whose seeds would develop a mildew-like covering that had an inebriating effect (thus, its Latin name, *ebriacum*). This grass grows wild and thus impedes the development of wheat. Jesus's well-known parable of the tares uses this image as a symbol of wickedness that contends with goodness.

ABOUT THE AUTHOR

GIANFRANCO CARDINAL RAVASI currently serves in the Roman Curia as President of the *Pontifical Council for Culture*. He studied at the Pontifical Gregorian University and at the Pontifical Biblical Institute. He taught the Old Testament at the theological faculty of northern Italy. From 1989 to 2007 he served as prefect of the Ambrosian Library in Milan. Cardinal Ravasi has written many books, articles for *L'Osservatore Romano* and *L'Avvenire*, and hosts the television show *Frontiers of the Spirit*. He is especially known for his interest in the conversation between faith and the modern world.

ABOUT THE PUBLISHER

The CROSSROAD PUBLISHING COMPANY publishes CROSSROAD and HERDER & HERDER books. We offer a 200-year global family tradition of books on spiritual living and religious thought. We promote reading as a time-tested discipline for focus and understanding. We help authors shape, clarify, write, and effectively promote their ideas. We select, edit, and distribute books. With our expertise and passion we provide wholesome spiritual nourishment for heart, mind, and soul through the written word.

You May Also Like

Niklaus Brantschen
Fasting
What · Why · How

Providing a no-nonsense introduction to fasting, this guide presents the physical, spiritual, and sociopolitical dimensions of this ancient practice. Short reflections from practitioners clarify misunderstandings about what fasting is and is not. The inclusion of a practical overview of the steps to conducting a fast round out a thorough exploration of a venerated practice.

Paperback, 112 pages, 978-0-8245-2540-8

Hellmut Luetzner, M.D.
The New Life Fasting Guide
Seven Days to a Healthier, Happier You

Written by one of Europe's most experienced and renowned fasting doctors, this step-by-step reference provides daily guidance to complete a seven-day fast. The guidebook addresses a myriad of topics associated with fasting, including its history, common and successful forms, losing weight, overcoming temptations, and recipes for reintroducing food into the body.

Paperback, 124 pages, 978-0-8245-2260-3

Lorenzo Albacete
God at the Ritz
Attraction to Infinity

Lorenzo Albacete, a close friend of Pope John Paul II, physicist, and *New York Times* columnist, shows that religion has a place amid conversations on science and contemporary culture. With humor and honesty, Albacete answers questions about life and death, good and evil, science and religion, religion and politics, and other issues.

Paperback, 208 pages, 978-0-8245-2472-2

Support your local bookstore or order
directly from the publisher at www.crossroadpublishing.com.
To request a catalog or inquire about
quantity orders, e-mail sales@crossroadpublishing.com.

The Crossroad Publishing Company

www.ingramcontent.com/pod-product-compliance
Lightning Source LLC
LaVergne TN
LVHW030633080426
835509LV00022B/3464

* 9 7 8 0 8 2 4 5 2 1 8 2 0 *